German Genealogy Research Online

Tips and Links

Compiled by Leland K. Meitzler

**Online German Gazetteers
FamilySearch.org German Databases
Translating Online German Websites
International Genealogical Index (IGI) Online
Full German State Archives Addresses & Contact Information
Finding Pictures, Images, and Websites for Your Ancestral Home**

Including 30 Helpful Online German Research Resources

German Genealogy Research Online - Tips and Links

A Supplement to *The German Researcher, 4th Edition*, by Fay & Douglas Dearden

Compiled by Leland K. Meitzler

Copyright 2012

Published by Family Roots Publishing Co., LLC

PO Box 830, Bountiful, Utah 84011

Tel: 801-992-3705, Fax 815-642-0103

Email: Leland@FamilyRootsPublishing.com

www.familyrootspublishing.com

www.genealogyblog.com

ISBN 13: 978-1-933194-98-1

ISBN 10: 1-933194-98-7

Item # FR0120

Printed and Bound in the United States of America

Table of Contents

Introduction

I began my quest for my German ancestors in the pre-Internet era. Searching for the birthplace of my great-grandfather, Karl Meitzler (1820-1899) was my first challenge. When I found his place of birth (Kriegsfeld, Bavaria) in an old county history, I was off and running. Most of my early research was slow, in that I spent many hours writing letters, and waiting for documents to arrive.

When I eventually had the opportunity to travel, I began to make my way to the LDS Family History Library in Salt Lake City, searching through their tremendous collections, and printing reams of church & civil vital records found in microfilmed records. I spent hours gazing at microfiche International Genealogical Index record extractions in the Library, making notes and following up with more searches of the microfilm. Much of this I still do today. I just don't write as many letters, and I use the Internet for searches of the IGI.

This booklet is written to give the genealogical researcher a quick reference guide to some of the most important German genealogy research uses of the Internet. It's not meant to be comprehensive. However, it does include what I believe to be the most important websites for anyone getting started in using the web in their search for German ancestors.

I've also included a number of sections on how I've used the Internet to broaden my knowledge of not only my ancestors, but the places where they lived, finding not only thousands of pictures, but detailed information about the history and geography of those places.

Although much of my Germanic research is the same today as it was a decade ago, the Internet has become an important part of my research. I'm confident that it will be the same way for you.

We now have many online databases available to us, with everything from maps & gazetteers to vital records, accessible with just a few keystrokes. Correspondence with foreign archives, churches, and cousins is certainly much faster using email, than writing a letter and waiting.... The ability to automatically translate websites and emails (albeit a bit stilted) makes doing foreign research much easier than it was previously.

In the last decade many of the German state archives have either moved and/or changed their mailing addresses. Virtually all of them now have websites, and can be contacted by email. For this reason, I've included a full listing of the German state archives, with current contact information.

Finally, I've included the names and the links to 30 of what I believe to be the most important websites available for helping with our German research. Again, it's by no means comprehensive, but I find that these are the sites that I keep going back to, again and again, and I recommend them to you.

Finding Pictures, Images, and Websites for Your Ancestral Home

Start out by searching the Internet with Google Images <www.google.com/imghp>. Plan to revisit this site regularly.

Search for the name of the village or city where your ancestor lived. In my case, I just typed "Kriegsfeld" into the search box – and got an immediate 41,700 pictures – most of Kreigsfeld, Germany.

Then I typed "Kriegsfield, Germany," getting 367 results.

I tried "Kriegsfeld, Deutschland," with 8,960 results.

Next I tried "Kriegsfeld, Pfalz," getting 31,200 results.

Searching for "Kriegsfeld Church" got 2,980 hits (from an American or English point of view), while searching for "Kriegsfeld Kirche" brought 27,200 results from a German viewpoint.

Many municipalities, cities, towns, and districts have websites of their own. Just type the place name in the Google search box at <www.google.com>, and see what you can find.

Translating Online German Websites

The Google Chrome browser has an automatic translation feature, allowing the user to set it up to automatically translate foreign language pages.

Get the free Google Chrome browser at: <www.google.com/intl/en/chrome/browser/>

If you're using another browser, you may get a "Translate This Page?" link when the page opens. If you don't get the link, do the following:

Highlight and copy the website address (URL) of the foreign language page.

Open Google Translate: <http://translate.google.com>

Paste the website address (URL) into the "Translate" box.

Click on "Translate."

FamilySearch.org German Databases

As of October 3, 2012, the German Historical Records Collection contained 33 collections, ten of them indexed (see below). Twenty-nine of the collections were made up of digitized images. This collection continues to grow.

The site includes three databases of German Vital Records (Births, Baptisms, Marriages, Deaths, and Burials, containing over nearly 50 million records dating from 1558 to 1958).

COLLECTION	RECORDS
Germany, Births and Baptisms, 1558-1898	37,703,414
Germany, Marriages, 1558-1929	8,521,370
Germany, Deaths and Burials, 1582-1958	3,507,357
Germany, Baden, Church Book Duplicates, 1810-1869	107,547
Germany, Bremen Passenger Depart. Lists, 1904-1914	44,315
Germany, Mecklenburg-Schwerin Census, 1867	105,115
Germany, Mecklenburg-Schwerin Census, 1890	94,251
Germany, Mecklenburg-Schwerin Census, 1900	733,518
Germany, Prussia, Brandenburg and Posen, Church Book Duplicates, 1794-1874	1,675,056
Germany, Westfalen, Minden Citizen Lists, 1574-1902	14,707

See all databases at the following URL:
<https://familysearch.org/search/collection/list#page=1&countryId=1927074>

FamilySearch.org
International Genealogical Index (IGI) Online

The International Genealogical Index originated as an early family history database that listed several hundred million names of deceased persons from throughout the world. It contains data on millions of Germanic individuals.

The data came from two sources. The Community Indexed IGI, made up of vital and church records from the early 1500s to 1885 – and the Community Contributed IGI, made up of personal family information submitted to the LDS Church.

Although both databases are valuable, the data in the Community Indexed IGI is by far the most authoritative, as it is extracted vital record data, and not just submitted (often incorrect or incomplete) information.

The IGI is now available online at: <www.familysearch.org/search/collection/igi/?icid=fsHome IGICollection>

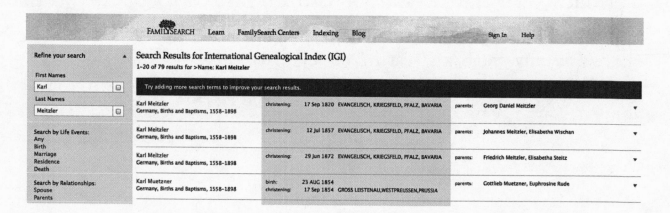

Online German Surname Distribution Maps

If you can't find any place of origin for your German ancestor in the old country, you might try using current surname distribution maps to see where your surname is found in Germany today.

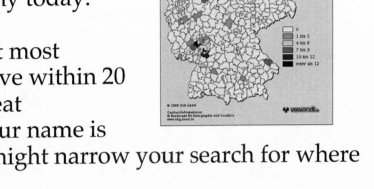

For example, I've found that most Meitzlers in Germany still live within 20 or 30 miles of where my Great Grandfather was born. If your name is uncommon, this approach might narrow your search for where your people came from.

There are a number of surname distribution map sites online. Following are three common ones, two are free and the other is Ancestry.de to which many of us have subscriptions.

Geogen Surname Mapping – Free
<http://christoph.stoepel.net/geogen/en/Default.aspx>

Ancestry.de Namensforschung – $ Subscription service:
<www.ancestry.de/learn/learningcenters/facts.aspx>. Once you've logged in, click on the link, getting the Infocenter, & under Namensforschung, enter your Familienname (Surname). Click "Start." The surname distribution map will come up.

Verwandt.de German Surname Maps – Free
<www.verwandt.de/karten/> This site is the German version of dynastree.com. This site gives more detailed information about the families and where they live.

Online German Gazetteers

Michael Rademacher's Germany-Austria Ortsbuch 1871-1990:
<www.verwaltungsgeschichte.de/ortsbuch39.html>

The German gazetteers at FallingRain.com:
<www.fallingrain.com/world/GM/>

German Gazetteers Online, by Kory L. Meyerink:
<www.progenealogists.com/germangazetteersonline.htm>

Google Earth: <www.google.com/earth/index.html>. It's not a gazetteer, but certainly can be used like one.

Meyers Orts- und Verkehrs-Lexikon des Deutschen Reichs:
<http://search.ancestry.com/Browse/list.aspx?dbid=1074>

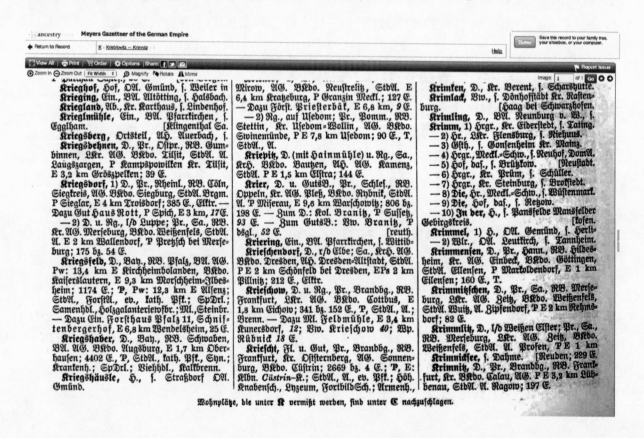

German State Archives – Addresses & Contact Information

This data updates the addresses located on pages 46 & 47 of "The German Researcher"

Alsace-Lorraine
Departmental Archives of the Bas-Rhin
Archives départementales du Bas-Rhin

Physical & Postal Address:
5, rue Fischart
67000 Strasbourg
France
Tel: 03 69 06 73 06
E-Mail: archives@cg67.fr
<http://archives.cg67.fr/index.asp>

Anhalt, see: Sachsen-Anhalt

Baden, see: Baden-Württemberg

Baden-Württemberg
National Archive of Baden-Württemberg
Landesarchiv Baden-Württemberg

Physical & Postal Address:
Nördliche Hildapromenade 3
D-76133 Karlsruhe
Germany
Tel: 0721/926-2206
Fax: 0721/926-2231
E-Mail: glakarlsruhe@la-bw.de
<www.landesarchiv-bw.de/web/>

Bayern (Bavaria)
Bavarian State Archives
Die Staatlichen Archive in Bayern

Generaldirektion der Staatlichen Archive Bayerns
Schönfeldstr. 5
80539 München
Germany
Tel.: +49 89/28638-2482
Fax: +49 89/28638-2615
E-mail: poststelle@gda.bayern.de
<www.gda.bayern.de/index.php>

Berlin
The Prussian Privy State Archives
Geheimes Staatsarchiv Preußischer
Kulturbesitz (GStA PK)

Physical & Postal Address
Archivstraße 12-14
D-14195 Berlin (Dahlem)
GermanyTel: 030/266 44 75 00
Fax: 030/266 44 31 26
E-Mail: gsta.pk@gsta.spk-berlin.de
<www.gsta.spk-berlin.de/index.html>

Brandenburg
Brandenburg State Archives
Brandenburgisches Landeshauptarchiv

Physical Address
Zum Windmühlenberg
14469 Potsdam, OT Bornim
Germany

Postal Address
Postfach 600449
14469 Potsdam, OT Bornim
Germany
Tel: 0331 5674-0
Fax: 0331 5674-212
E-Mail: poststelle@blha.brandenburg.de
<www.landeshauptarchiv-brandenburg.de>

Bremen (City-State)
State Archive of Bremen
Staatsarchiv Bremen

Physical & Postal Address
Am Staatsarchiv 1
28203 Bremen
Germany
Tel: 0421 / 361-6221
Fax: 0421 / 361-10247
E-Mail: office@staatsarchiv.bremen.de

Braunschwig (Brunswick), see: Niedersachsen

Hamburg (City-State)
Hamburg State Archives
Staatsarchiv Hamburg

Physical & Postal Address
Kattunbleiche 19
22041 Hamburg
Germany
Tel: 040-428 31 – 3200
poststelle@kb.hamburg.de
poststelle@staatsarchiv.hamburg.de
<www.hamburg.de/staatsarchiv/>

Hannover, see: Niedersachsen

Hessen (Hesse)
Hessian State Archives
Hessisches Hauptstaatsarchiv

Physical & Postal Address
Mosbacher Straße 55
65187 Wiesbaden
Germany
Tel: +49 (0) 611 8 81-0
Fax: +49 (0) 611 8 81-1 45
E-Mail: Poststelle@hhstaw.hessen.de

Hessen Nassau, see: Rheinland and Niedersachsen

Hohenzollern, see: Baden-Württemberg

Lippe
East Westphalia-Lippe National Archives
(Formerly National Archives Detmold)
Landesarchiv Nordrhein-Westfalen
Abteilung Ostwestfalen-Lippe

Physical & Postal Address
Willi-Hofmann-Straße 2
D-32756 Detmold
Germany
Tel: 05231-766-0
Fax: 05231-766-114
E-Mail: owl@lav.nrw.de

Lübeck, see: Schleswig-Holstein

Mecklenburg
Provincial Archives of Mecklenburg-Vorpommern (Schwerin State Archives)
Landesarchiv Entdeke Mecklenburg-Vorpommern

Physical & Mailing Address
Graf-Schack-Allee 2,
D-19053 Schwerin
Germany
Tel: 0385-588794 10
Fax: 0385-588794 12
Email: poststelle@landeshauptarchiv-schwerin.de

Niedersachsen (Lower Saxony)
Lower Saxony State Archives
des Niedersächsischen Landesarchivs

Lower Saxony State Archives – Central Archives Administration
Niedersächsisches Landesarchiv – Zentrale Archivverwaltung
Am Archiv 1
D-30169 Hannover
Germany
Tel.: 0511-120 6601
Fax: 0511-120 6639
E-Mail: poststelle@nla.niedersachsen.de

Lower Saxony State Archives – Aurich
Niedersächsisches Landesarchiv – Staatsarchiv Aurich
Oldersumer Straße 50
26603 Aurich
Germany
Tel: (04941) 176 660
Fax: (04941) 176 673
E-mail: Aurich@nla.niedersachsen.de

Lower Saxony State Archives – Bückeburg
Niedersächsisches Landesarchiv – Staatsarchiv Bückeburg
Schloßplatz 2
31675 Bückeburg
Germany
Tel: (05722) 9677-30
Fax: (05722) 1289
E-Mail: Bueckeburg@nla.niedersachsen.de

Lower Saxony State Archives – Hanover
Niedersächsisches Landesarchiv – Hauptstaatsarchiv Hannover
Am Archiv 1
30169 Hannover
Germany
Tel: (0511) 120-6601
Fax: (0511) 120-6699
E-Mail: Hannover@nla.niedersachsen.de

Niedersächsisches Landesarchiv – Staatsarchiv Oldenburg
Lower Saxony State Archives – Oldenburg
Damm 43
26135 Oldenburg
Germany
Tel: (0441) 92 44 100
Fax: (0441) 92 44 292
E-Mail: Oldenburg@nla.niedersachsen.de

Lower Saxony State Archives – Osnabrück
Niedersächsisches Landesarchiv – Staatsarchiv Osnabrück
Schloßstr. 29
49074 Osnabrück
Germany
Tel: (0541) 33162-0
Fax: (0541) 33162-62
E-Mail: Osnabrueck@nla.niedersachsen.de

Lower Saxony State Archives – Stade
Niedersächsisches Landesarchiv – Staatsarchiv Stade
Am Sande 4c
21682 Stade
Germany
Tel: (04141) 406-404
Fax: (04141) 406-400
E-Mail: Stade@nla.niedersachsen.de

Lower Saxony State Archives – Wolfenbütte
Niedersächsisches Landesarchiv – Staatsarchiv Wolfenbüttel
Forstweg 2
38302 Wolfenbüttel
Germany
Tel: (05331) 935-0
Fax: (05331) 935-211
E-mail: Wolfenbuettel@nla.niedersachsen.de

Nordrhein-Westfalen (North Rhine Westphalia), see also: Rheinland

Nordrhein-Westfalen State Archives
Landesarchiv NRW

Physical & Mailing Address
Graf-Adolf-Straße 67
D-40210 Düsseldorf
Germany
Tel: +49 211 159238-0
Fax: +49 211 159238-111
E-Mail: poststelle@lav.nrw.de
<www.archive.nrw.de/lav/index.php>

Oldenburg, see: Niedersachsen (Lower Saxony) – Lower Saxony State Archives – Oldenburg

Ostpreussen (East Prussia)
The Prussian Privy State Archives
Geheimes Staatsarchiv Preußischer Kulturbesitz (GStA PK)

Physical & Postal Address
Archivstraße 12-14
D-14195 Berlin (Dahlem)
Germany
Tel: 030/266 44 75 00
Fax: 030/266 44 31 26
E-Mail: gsta.pk@gsta.spk-berlin.de
<www.gsta.spk-berlin.de/index.html>

Pfalz (Palatinate)
Rheinland Pfalz Provincial Archives Speyer
Rheinland Pfalz Landesarchiv Speyer

Physical & Postal Address
Otto-Mayer-Str. 9
D-67346 Speyer
Germany
Tel: 06232 9192-0
Telefax: 06232 9192-100
E-Mail: post@landesarchiv-speyer.de

Pommern (Pomerania)
The Association of East German Genealogists (AGoFF)
Research Center of Pomerania
Die Arbeitsgemeinschaft ostdeutscher Familienforscher e. V. (AGoFF)
Forschungsstelle Pommern

Physical & Postal Address
Elmar Bruhn - Leitung der Forschungsstelle (head of the research unit)
Lohkamp 13
D-22117 Hamburg
Germany
Tel: 040-7127073
<http://agoff.de/fst/pom.htm>

Poznan/Posen (Poland)
The State Archive in Poznan
Archiwum Państwowe w Poznan

Physical & Postal Address
ul. 23 Lutego 41/43
60-967 Poznanskrytka pocztowa 546
Poland
Phone: (+48) (61) 852 46 01 to 03
Fax: (+48) (61) 851 73 10
E-mail: archiwum@poznan.ap.gov.pl
<www.poznan.ap.gov.pl/?

Rheinland (Rhine Province)
NRW State Archives – Brühl
Landesarchiv Nordrhein-Westfalen
Abteilung Rheinland – Brühl

Physical & Postal Address
Schloßstr. 10-12
D-50321 Brühl (Rhein-Erft-Kreis)
Germany

Note - The archive is located in a wing of the Schloss Augustusburg castle.
Tel: 02232/ 94538-0
Fax: 02232/ 94538-38
E-Mail: rheinland-bruehl@lav.nrw.de

Saarland (Saar)
National Archives of Saarland
Archiv des Saarlandes

Physical & Postal Address
Dudweilerstraße 1
D-66133 Saarbrücken-Scheidt
Germany
Tel: (0681) 501-00 (State Government Switchboard)
Fax (0681) 501-1933
E-Mail: landesarchiv@landesarchiv.saarland.de
<www.saarland.de/landesarchiv.htm>

Sachsen (Saxony)
Saxon State Archives
Sächsisches Staatsarchiv

Physical & Postal Address
Archivstr. 14
D-01097 Dresden
Germany
Tel: +49 351/89219-710
Fax: +49 351/89219-709
poststelle@sta.smi.sachsen.de

Sachsen-Anhalt (Saxony-Anhalt)
State Archive of Saxony-Anhalt –
Magdeburg
Landeshauptarchiv Sachsen-Anhalt –
Magdeburg

Physical and Postal Address
Brück Straße 2
D-39114 Magdeburg
Germany
Tel: 0391/59806-0 (Central)
Fax: 0391/59806-600
E-Mail: poststelle@lha.mi.sachsen-anhalt.de
<www.sachsen-anhalt.de/index.php?id=32012>

Schaumberg-Lippe, see: Niedersachsen

Schlesien (Silesia)
Silesia Research Center
The Association of East German
Genealogists (AGoFF)
Research Centre Silesia
Die Arbeitsgemeinschaft ostdeutscher
Familienforscher e. V. (AGoFF)

Physical and Postal Address
Andreas Rösler
Kaskelstraße 41
D-10317 Berlin
Germany
<http://agoff.de/fst/schl.htm>

Schleswig-Holstein
Schleswig-Holstein State Archives
Landesarchiv Schleswig-Holstein

Physical and Postal Address
Prinzenpalais
D-24837 Schleswig
Germany
Tel: +49 4621 8618-00
Fax: +49 4621 8618-01
E-Mail: landesarchiv@la.landsh.de
<www.schleswig-holstein.de/LA/EN/LA_node.html>

Thüringen (Thuringia), see also: Sachsen
The Thuringia State Archives
Die Staatsarchive in Thüringen

Thuringia State Archives – Altenburg
Staatsarchiv Altenburg

Physical Address
Schloß 7
D-04600 Altenburg
Germany

Postal Address
PF 13 31
D-04583 Altenburg
Germany
Tel: 0 34 47 / 31 54 88
Fax: 0 34 47 / 50 49 29
<www.thueringen.de/de/staatsarchive/>

Thuringia State Archives – Gotha
Staatsarchiv Gotha

Physical Address
PF 10 04 24
D-99854 Gotha
Germany

Postal Address
Schloß Friedenstein
D-99867 Gotha
Germany
Tel: +49 (0) 36 21 / 30 27 90
Fax: +49 (0) 36 21 / 30 27 947

Thuringia State Archives – Greiz
Staatsarchiv Greiz

Physical & Postal Address
Friedhofstraße 1a
D-07973 Greiz
Germany
Tel: +49 (0) 36 61 / 25 37
Fax: +49 (0) 36 61 / 68 98 69

Thuringia State Archives – Meiningen

Staatsarchiv Meiningen

Physical Address
Schloß Bibrabau
D-98617 Meiningen
Germany

Archivdepot Suhl:
Neundorfer Straße 10-12
D-98527 Suhl
Germany

Postal Address
PF 10 06 54
D-98606 Meiningen
Germany

Meiningen Phone & Fax:
Tel: +49 (0) 36 93 / 44 67 0
Fax: +49 (0) 36 93 / 50 22 18

Suhl Phone & Fax:
Tel: +49 (0) 36 81 / 75 73-0
Fax: +49 (0) 36 81 / 75 73 33

Thuringia State Archives – Rudolstadt
Staatsarchiv Rudolstadt

Physical & Postal Address
Schloß Heidecksburg
D-07407 Rudolstadt
Germany
Tel: +49 (0) 36 72 / 43 19-0
Fax: +49 (0) 36 72 / 43 19 31
E-mail: rudolstadt@staatsarchive.thueringen.de

Thuringia State Archives – Weimer
Staatsarchiv Weimer

Physical Address
Marstallstraße 2
D-99423 Weimar
Germany

Postal Address
PF 27 26
D-99408 Weimar
Germany

Marstallstraße 2
Records from 1920
Tel: +49 (0) 36 43 / 870-0
Fax: +49 (0) 36 43 / 870-100

Beethovenplatz 3

Records before 1920
Tel: +49 (0) 36 43 / 87 198-315
Fax: +49 (0) 36 43 / 87 198-350

Note: Thuringia is made up of: Reuss-Greiz, Reuss-Greiz-Gera, Saxe-Altenburg, Sachsen-Koburg-Gotha, Sachsen-Meiningen, Sachsen-Weimer-Eisenach, Schwarzburg-Rudolstadt, and Schwarzburg-Sonderhausen.

Waldeck, see: Niedersachsen and Hessen

Westfalen (Westphalia), see also: Niedersachsen & Rheinland
FO Archives of Westpahlia
LWL Archivamt für Westfalen

Physical Address
Jahnstraße 26
D-48147 Münster
Germany

Postal Address
LWL-Archivamt für Westfalen
D-48133 Münster
Germany
Tel: 0251 / 591-3890
Fax: 0251 / 591-269
E-Mail: LWL-Archivamt@lwl.org
<www.lwl.org/LWL/Kultur/Archivamt>

Westpreussen, see: Ostpreussen (East Prussia)

Württemberg
State Archives of Baden-Württemberg: Stuttgart
Landesarchiv Baden-Württemberg: Hauptstaatsarchiv Stuttgart

Physical & Postal Address
Konrad-Adenauer-Straße 4
D-70173 Stuttgart
Germany
Tel: 0711 / 212-4335
Fax: 0711 / 212-4360
E-Mail: hstastuttgart@la-bw.de
<www.landesarchiv-bw.de/web/49689>

30 Helpful Online German Research Resources

Ancestry.com World Explorer Membership -$- Annual & Monthly memberships are available. The membership allows access to the data found at other Ancestry sites, including Ancestry.de <www.ancestry.de> – the German Ancestry website. <www.ancestry.com/subscribe/products/?p=world_deluxe>

Archives in Germany, by Andreas Hanacek: <http://home.bawue.de/~hanacek/info/earchive.htm>

Castle Garden – America's First Immigration Center: <www.castlegarden.org>

Cyndi's List Germany/Deutschland links: <www.cyndislist.com/germany/>

Deciphering German Script (FamilySearch): <www.familysearch.org/learn/wiki/en/Deciphering_German_Script_1-12>

Ellis Island Website: <www.ellisisland.org>

FamilySearch Catalog: <www.familysearch.org/#form=catalog>

FEEFHS Map Library: <www.feefhs.org/maplibrary.html>

Genealogy.net, the German Genealogy Portal: <www.genealogienetz.de/genealogy.html>

German Church Book Portal: <www.kirchenbuchportal.de/>

Germany Church Records (FamilySearch Wiki): <https://familysearch.org/learn/wiki/en/Germany_Church_Records>

German Genealogy Group: <http://germangenealogygroup.com>

German Genealogy Research Guidebooks (also see *Map Guide to German Parish Registers* below): <www.familyrootspublishing.com/store/category.php?cat=14>

Germany GenWeb Project: <www.rootsweb.ancestry.com/~wggerman/>

German Script Tutorial (BYU): <http://script.byu.edu/german/en/welcome.aspx>

German Telephone Book: <www.dastelefonbuch.de>

Google Search: Search for information on your ancestral home at <www.google.com>

Google Images: You can also find photos of German villages by searching at <http://images.google.com/>

Google Translate: <http://translate.google.com>

Hamburg Passenger Lists info with links at FamilySearch Wiki: <https://familysearch.org/learn/wiki/en/Hamburg_Passenger_Lists>

Joe Beine's German Roots German Genealogy website: <www.germanroots.com>

Library of Congress European Reading Room – The Germans in America: <www.loc.gov/rr/european/imde/germany.html>

Map Guide to German Parish Registers: The place-name index, as well as descriptions & ordering information to each of these books is posted online at <www.familyrootspublishing.com/store/category.php?cat=163>

Palatines to America National German Genealogy Society: <www.palam.org>

Perry-Casteñada Library European Map Collection: <www.lib.utexas.edu/maps/historical/history_europe.html>

ProGenealogists German Genealogy Links: <www.progenealogists.com/germany/germangenealogylinks.htm>

Polish State and Ecclesiastical Archives: Their Addresses, Locations and Websites, by Tadeusz Hubert Pilat: <www.progenealogists.com/poland/archives.htm>

Staedte-Verlag Maps:

Successful Genealogical Correspondence and Travel to Germany, by Friedrich R. Wollmershäuser: <www.progenealogists.com/germany/articles/gertravel.htm>

Writing Letters to Germany – German language form letters: <www.genealogyforum.com/gfaol/resource/German/letter.htm>

About the Author

Leland Meitzler loves genealogy, as well as the subject of history in general. He also likes to blog, and GenealogyBlog.com is the product of that passion. He started blogging in 2003. The Meitzlers founded *Heritage Quest* in 1985, and he worked as managing editor of that periodical through 2005. Leland then worked as the managing editor of *The Genealogical Helper* from 2006 until 2009. Besides writing for GenealogyBlog, Leland is the manager of Family Roots Publishing Co., LLC – specializing in the publication and marketing of genealogy guidebooks. He also edits the email periodical, *Genealogy Newsline*. Leland has given over 2,000 lectures on genealogical subjects to national, state and local genealogical groups. Leland, and Donna Potter Phillips direct the annual Salt Lake Christmas Tour each December, the first annual tour being in 1985.

Anton Kimpfler
Christening Date 1872 May 27
 Birth   May 26 1872
FATHER Joseph Kimpfler
Mother Benedicta Heberger